# Seeking Out the
# Mythical Unicorn!

## A Monthly Planner

## Activinotes

*Activinotes*

DAILY JOURNALS, PLANNERS, NOTEBOOKS AND OTHER BLANK BOOKS

# Monthly Planner

# Monthly Planner

# January

# Monthly Planner

| MONDAY | TUESDAY | WEDNESDAY |
|---|---|---|
| | | |
| THURSDAY | FRIDAY | SATURDAY |
| | | |

SUNDAY

# Monthly Planner

| MONDAY | TUESDAY | WEDNESDAY |
|---|---|---|
| | | |
| **THURSDAY** | **FRIDAY** | **SATURDAY** |
| | | |

SUNDAY

# Monthly Planner

| To Do | Reminder | To Buy |
|-------|----------|--------|

## Notes :

# Monthly Planner

| MONDAY | TUESDAY | WEDNESDAY |
|---|---|---|
| | | |
| **THURSDAY** | **FRIDAY** | **SATURDAY** |
| | | |

**SUNDAY**

# Monthly Planner

| MONDAY | TUESDAY | WEDNESDAY |
|---|---|---|
| | | |
| **THURSDAY** | **FRIDAY** | **SATURDAY** |
| | | |

SUNDAY

# Monthly Planner

| To Do | Reminder | To Buy |
|-------|----------|--------|

## Notes :

# Monthly Planner

# February

# Monthly Planner

| MONDAY | TUESDAY | WEDNESDAY |
|--------|---------|-----------|
|        |         |           |

| THURSDAY | FRIDAY | SATURDAY |
|----------|--------|----------|
|          |        |          |

SUNDAY

# Monthly Planner

| MONDAY | TUESDAY | WEDNESDAY |
|--------|---------|-----------|
|        |         |           |

| THURSDAY | FRIDAY | SATURDAY |
|----------|--------|----------|
|          |        |          |

SUNDAY

# Monthly Planner

| To Do | Reminder | To Buy |
|-------|----------|--------|
| | | |

**Notes:**

# Monthly Planner

| MONDAY | TUESDAY | WEDNESDAY |
|---|---|---|
| | | |
| THURSDAY | FRIDAY | SATURDAY |
| | | |

SUNDAY

# Monthly Planner

| MONDAY | TUESDAY | WEDNESDAY |
|---|---|---|
|  |  |  |
| THURSDAY | FRIDAY | SATURDAY |
|  |  |  |

SUNDAY

# Monthly Planner

| To Do | Reminder | To Buy |
|-------|----------|--------|
|       |          |        |

## Notes :

# Monthly Planner

# March

# Monthly Planner

| MONDAY | TUESDAY | WEDNESDAY |
|--------|---------|-----------|
|        |         |           |
| THURSDAY | FRIDAY | SATURDAY |
|          |        |          |

SUNDAY

# Monthly Planner

| MONDAY | TUESDAY | WEDNESDAY |
|--------|---------|-----------|
| | | |

| THURSDAY | FRIDAY | SATURDAY |
|----------|--------|----------|
| | | |

SUNDAY

# Monthly Planner

| To Do | Reminder | To Buy |
|-------|----------|--------|

## Notes :

# Monthly Planner

| MONDAY | TUESDAY | WEDNESDAY |
|---|---|---|
| | | |
| **THURSDAY** | **FRIDAY** | **SATURDAY** |
| | | |

SUNDAY

# Monthly Planner

| MONDAY | TUESDAY | WEDNESDAY |
|--------|---------|-----------|
| | | |

| THURSDAY | FRIDAY | SATURDAY |
|----------|--------|----------|
| | | |

**SUNDAY**

# Monthly Planner

| To Do | Reminder | To Buy |
|---|---|---|
|  |  |  |

**Notes :**

# Monthly Planner

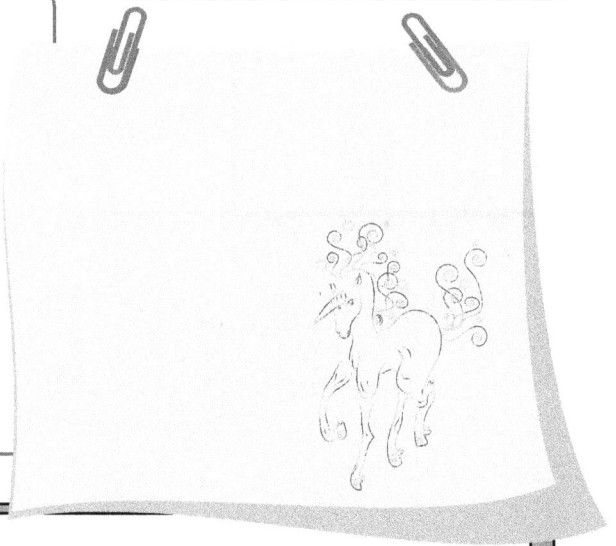

---
---
---
---

# April

# Monthly Planner

| MONDAY | TUESDAY | WEDNESDAY |
|---|---|---|
| | | |
| **THURSDAY** | **FRIDAY** | **SATURDAY** |
| | | |

| SUNDAY |
|---|
| |

# Monthly Planner

| MONDAY | TUESDAY | WEDNESDAY |
|---|---|---|
| | | |
| THURSDAY | FRIDAY | SATURDAY |
| | | |

SUNDAY

# Monthly Planner

| To Do | Reminder | To Buy |
|---|---|---|
|  |  |  |

Notes :

# Monthly Planner

| MONDAY | TUESDAY | WEDNESDAY |
|---|---|---|
| | | |

| THURSDAY | FRIDAY | SATURDAY |
|---|---|---|
| | | |

| SUNDAY |
|---|
| |

# Monthly Planner

| MONDAY | TUESDAY | WEDNESDAY |
|---|---|---|
| | | |
| THURSDAY | FRIDAY | SATURDAY |
| | | |

SUNDAY

# Monthly Planner

| To Do | Reminder | To Buy |
|-------|----------|--------|

Notes :

# Monthly Planner

_____

_____

_____

_____

# may

# Monthly Planner

| MONDAY | TUESDAY | WEDNESDAY |
|---|---|---|
| | | |
| **THURSDAY** | **FRIDAY** | **SATURDAY** |
| | | |

SUNDAY

# Monthly Planner

| MONDAY | TUESDAY | WEDNESDAY |
|---|---|---|
| | | |

| THURSDAY | FRIDAY | SATURDAY |
|---|---|---|
| | | |

SUNDAY

# Monthly Planner

| To Do | Reminder | To Buy |
|-------|----------|--------|

## Notes:

# Monthly Planner

| MONDAY | TUESDAY | WEDNESDAY |
|--------|---------|-----------|
|        |         |           |

| THURSDAY | FRIDAY | SATURDAY |
|----------|--------|----------|
|          |        |          |

**SUNDAY**

# Monthly Planner

| MONDAY | TUESDAY | WEDNESDAY |
|--------|---------|-----------|
|        |         |           |

| THURSDAY | FRIDAY | SATURDAY |
|----------|--------|----------|
|          |        |          |

SUNDAY

# Monthly Planner

| To Do | Reminder | To Buy |
|---|---|---|
|  |  |  |

### Notes :

# Monthly Planner

# June

# Monthly Planner

| MONDAY | TUESDAY | WEDNESDAY |
|--------|---------|-----------|
| | | |
| THURSDAY | FRIDAY | SATURDAY |
| | | |

SUNDAY

# Monthly Planner

| MONDAY | TUESDAY | WEDNESDAY |
|--------|---------|-----------|
| | | |
| **THURSDAY** | **FRIDAY** | **SATURDAY** |
| | | |

**SUNDAY**

# Monthly Planner

| To Do | Reminder | To Buy |
|---|---|---|
| | | |

## Notes :

# Monthly Planner

| MONDAY | TUESDAY | WEDNESDAY |
|---|---|---|
| | | |
| THURSDAY | FRIDAY | SATURDAY |
| | | |

SUNDAY

# Monthly Planner

| MONDAY | TUESDAY | WEDNESDAY |
|---|---|---|
| | | |
| THURSDAY | FRIDAY | SATURDAY |
| | | |

SUNDAY

# Monthly Planner

| To Do | Reminder | To Buy |
|-------|----------|--------|
|  |  |  |

Notes :

# Monthly Planner

# July

# Monthly Planner

| MONDAY | TUESDAY | WEDNESDAY |
|--------|---------|-----------|
| | | |

| THURSDAY | FRIDAY | SATURDAY |
|----------|--------|----------|
| | | |

SUNDAY

# Monthly Planner

| MONDAY | TUESDAY | WEDNESDAY |
|---|---|---|
|  |  |  |

| THURSDAY | FRIDAY | SATURDAY |
|---|---|---|
|  |  |  |

SUNDAY

# Monthly Planner

| To Do | Reminder | To Buy |
|-------|----------|--------|

**Notes :**

# Monthly Planner

| MONDAY | TUESDAY | WEDNESDAY |
|--------|---------|-----------|
|        |         |           |
| THURSDAY | FRIDAY | SATURDAY |
|          |        |          |

SUNDAY

# Monthly Planner

| MONDAY | TUESDAY | WEDNESDAY |
|---|---|---|
| | | |
| THURSDAY | FRIDAY | SATURDAY |
| | | |

SUNDAY

# Monthly Planner

| To Do | Reminder | To Buy |
|-------|----------|--------|
|  |  |  |

### Notes :

# Monthly Planner

# August

# Monthly Planner

| MONDAY | TUESDAY | WEDNESDAY |
|--------|---------|-----------|
| | | |

| THURSDAY | FRIDAY | SATURDAY |
|----------|--------|----------|
| | | |

| SUNDAY |
|--------|
| |

# Monthly Planner

| MONDAY | TUESDAY | WEDNESDAY |
|---|---|---|
| | | |
| **THURSDAY** | **FRIDAY** | **SATURDAY** |
| | | |

SUNDAY

# Monthly Planner

| To Do | Reminder | To Buy |
|---|---|---|
| | | |

## Notes :

# Monthly Planner

| MONDAY | TUESDAY | WEDNESDAY |
|--------|---------|-----------|
| | | |
| THURSDAY | FRIDAY | SATURDAY |
| | | |

SUNDAY

# Monthly Planner

| MONDAY | TUESDAY | WEDNESDAY |
|---|---|---|
| | | |
| THURSDAY | FRIDAY | SATURDAY |
| | | |

| SUNDAY |
|---|
| |

# Monthly Planner

| To Do | Reminder | To Buy |
|---|---|---|
|  |  |  |

## Notes :

# Monthly Planner

# September

# Monthly Planner

| MONDAY | TUESDAY | WEDNESDAY |
|---|---|---|
| | | |
| **THURSDAY** | **FRIDAY** | **SATURDAY** |
| | | |

SUNDAY

# Monthly Planner

| MONDAY | TUESDAY | WEDNESDAY |
|---|---|---|
| | | |

| THURSDAY | FRIDAY | SATURDAY |
|---|---|---|
| | | |

SUNDAY

# Monthly Planner

| To Do | Reminder | To Buy |
|-------|----------|--------|
|  |  |  |

Notes :

# Monthly Planner

| MONDAY | TUESDAY | WEDNESDAY |
|---|---|---|
| | | |
| **THURSDAY** | **FRIDAY** | **SATURDAY** |
| | | |

SUNDAY

# Monthly Planner

| MONDAY | TUESDAY | WEDNESDAY |
|---|---|---|
| | | |
| THURSDAY | FRIDAY | SATURDAY |
| | | |

SUNDAY

# Monthly Planner

| To Do | Reminder | To Buy |
|-------|----------|--------|

Notes :

# Monthly Planner

_____

_____

_____

_____

# October

# Monthly Planner

| MONDAY | TUESDAY | WEDNESDAY |
|---|---|---|
| | | |

| THURSDAY | FRIDAY | SATURDAY |
|---|---|---|
| | | |

SUNDAY

# Monthly Planner

| MONDAY | TUESDAY | WEDNESDAY |
|---|---|---|
| | | |
| **THURSDAY** | **FRIDAY** | **SATURDAY** |
| | | |

SUNDAY

# Monthly Planner

| To Do | Reminder | To Buy |
|-------|----------|--------|

## Notes:

# Monthly Planner

| MONDAY | TUESDAY | WEDNESDAY |
|--------|---------|-----------|
|        |         |           |

| THURSDAY | FRIDAY | SATURDAY |
|----------|--------|----------|
|          |        |          |

SUNDAY

# Monthly Planner

| MONDAY | TUESDAY | WEDNESDAY |
|---|---|---|
| | | |
| THURSDAY | FRIDAY | SATURDAY |
| | | |

SUNDAY

# Monthly Planner

| To Do | Reminder | To Buy |
|---|---|---|
| | | |

## Notes :

# Monthly Planner

# November

# Monthly Planner

| MONDAY | TUESDAY | WEDNESDAY |
|---|---|---|
| | | |
| THURSDAY | FRIDAY | SATURDAY |
| | | |

SUNDAY

# Monthly Planner

| MONDAY | TUESDAY | WEDNESDAY |
|---|---|---|
|  |  |  |

| THURSDAY | FRIDAY | SATURDAY |
|---|---|---|
|  |  |  |

SUNDAY

# Monthly Planner

| To Do | Reminder | To Buy |
|-------|----------|--------|

### Notes :

# Monthly Planner

| MONDAY | TUESDAY | WEDNESDAY |
|---|---|---|
| | | |

| THURSDAY | FRIDAY | SATURDAY |
|---|---|---|
| | | |

**SUNDAY**

# Monthly Planner

| MONDAY | TUESDAY | WEDNESDAY |
|---|---|---|
| | | |

| THURSDAY | FRIDAY | SATURDAY |
|---|---|---|
| | | |

SUNDAY

# Monthly Planner

| To Do | Reminder | To Buy |
|---|---|---|
|  |  |  |

## Notes :

# Monthly Planner

# December

# Monthly Planner

| MONDAY | TUESDAY | WEDNESDAY |
|---|---|---|
| | | |
| THURSDAY | FRIDAY | SATURDAY |
| | | |

SUNDAY

# Monthly Planner

| MONDAY | TUESDAY | WEDNESDAY |
|---|---|---|
| | | |
| **THURSDAY** | **FRIDAY** | **SATURDAY** |
| | | |

SUNDAY

# Monthly Planner

| To Do | Reminder | To Buy |
|-------|----------|--------|

## Notes :

# Monthly Planner

| MONDAY | TUESDAY | WEDNESDAY |
|---|---|---|
| | | |

| THURSDAY | FRIDAY | SATURDAY |
|---|---|---|
| | |  |

| SUNDAY |
|---|
| |

# Monthly Planner

| MONDAY | TUESDAY | WEDNESDAY |
|--------|---------|-----------|
|        |         |           |
| THURSDAY | FRIDAY | SATURDAY |
|          |        |          |

SUNDAY

# Monthly Planner

| To Do | Reminder | To Buy |
|---|---|---|
| | | |

## Notes:

# Monthly Planner

# Monthly Planner

# Monthly Planner

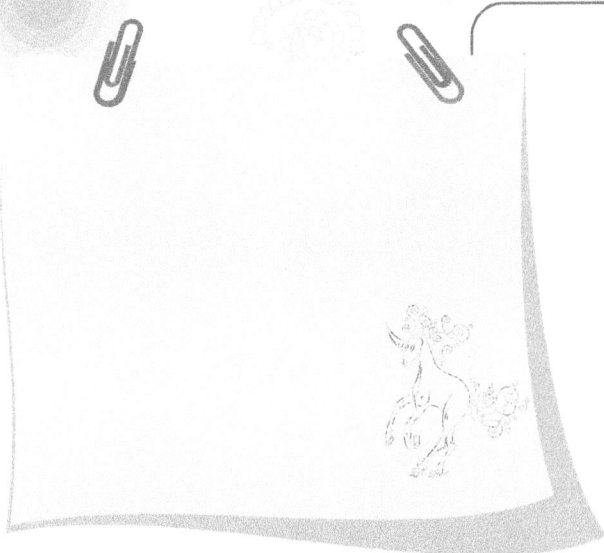

# Monthly Planner

# Notes

www.ingramcontent.com/pod-product-compliance
Lightning Source LLC
Chambersburg PA
CBHW081336090426

42737CB00017B/3167